Contents

Acknowledgments

Working on this, my first book, has been an exciting time. I have enjoyed working with Steve and greatly appreciate his special talents. This book was only made possible by the wonderful work of all the designers and homeowners who have so graciously permitted us to publish the photos of their work.

I wish to thank all my colleagues and associates who have assisted me in my quest to learn about kitchens. You know who you are. There are just so many to thank, I can't do it individually. I am grateful to the members of my family, who have always encouraged me to be whatever I wanted to be, with special thanks to my husband for his unwavering love and support.

Lastly, I would like to thank our editor, Jeff Snyder, my associate Chris Drieth, CKD, my sister, Edna L. Kimm, and my friend Kathy Vitello Fey for their input in this book. Their assistance has been irreplaceable.

— Laura M. Jensen, CMKBD

First and most importantly, I want to thank my lovely wife Rita, for her unending love, support, humor, assistance, styling, and for being the inspiration for everything that I do. Te Amo!

I want to also thank my mom & dad and my sisters; Mom and dad for their love and support, and for giving me a Midwest work ethic, and my sisters for being friends as well as family.

I have specialized in photographing kitchens and baths for over eight years; in that time I have shot more than 600 kitchens and 200 baths. I am deeply grateful to the extremely talented designers for allowing me to photograph their projects, and to the homeowners who have welcomed me into their homes. The great majority of my clients are members of the SEN Design Group. I want to publicly thank SEN's President, Ken Peterson, and his administrative staff for their support.

Finally, I have thoroughly enjoyed working on this project with Laura Jensen. She was able to take a mountain of photos and sculpt it into a book that we can both be proud of. It is great to work with someone who has such a vast body of knowledge and experience to draw from. Thanks also to Tina Skinner and Schiffer Publishing for taking a chance with us.

— Steven Paul Whitsitt

Photo courtesy of The Kitchen Guide, Inc., Barrington, IL

The Kitchen Guide

Laura M. Jensen, CMKBD
Photos by Steven Paul Whitsitt

Schiffer Publishing Ltd®

4880 Lower Valley Road Atglen, Pennsylvania 19310

Library of Congress Control Number: 2007937271

Designed by John P. Cheek
Cover design by Bruce Waters
Type set in Bernhard Modern BT/Zurich BT

ISBN: 978-0-7643-2889-3
Printed in China

Cover photo: *Photo courtesy of Thomas Lewis & Co., Lyons, CO*
Title page: *Photo courtesy of Kitchens by Teipen, Greenwood, IN*
Copyright page: *Photo courtesy of Kitchen & Bath Concepts of St. Simons, Inc. St. Simons Island, GA*
Contents page: *Photo courtesy of Kitchen Classics by Custom Crafters, Arlington, VA*
Acknowledgments page: *Photo courtesy of DCI Home Resources, Charlotte, NC*

Published by Schiffer Publishing Ltd.
4880 Lower Valley Road
Atglen, PA 19310
Phone: (610) 593-1777; Fax: (610) 593-2002
E-mail: Info@schifferbooks.com

For the largest selection of fine reference books on this and related subjects, please visit our web site at
www.schifferbooks.com
We are always looking for people to write books on new and related subjects. If you have an idea for a book please contact us at the above address.

This book may be purchased from the publisher.
Include $3.95 for shipping.
Please try your bookstore first.
You may write for a free catalog.

In Europe, Schiffer books are distributed by
Bushwood Books
6 Marksbury Ave.
Kew Gardens
Surrey TW9 4JF England
Phone: 44 (0) 20 8392-8585;
Fax: 44 (0) 20 8392-9876
E-mail: info@bushwoodbooks.co.uk
Website: www.bushwoodbooks.co.uk
Free postage in the U.K., Europe; air mail at cost.

Foreword

There are many kitchen idea books available today, but none more comprehensive, helpful, or inspirational than *The Kitchen Guide.* Indeed, it accomplishes three significant goals for its readers.

First, it performs the unique feat of capably assisting homeowners in visualizing what their dream kitchen will look like. The book is organized in an extraordinarily useful way where individual chapters focus on specific architectural elements, workstation designs, detail elements, and supplemental design concepts. Multiple photos of a particular design element vividly demonstrate its various applications, so homeowners are empowered to choose the look that best serves their needs.

Secondly, all the kitchens featured are the work of professional kitchen specialists. As a result, readers can be assured that the functional and aesthetic presentations are sound. When these design ideas are implemented in a similar fashion, homeowners will be thoroughly satisfied with the end results.

Finally, each kitchen, although selected to illustrate a certain design element, is loaded with many other wonderful design ideas. Take the time to enjoy each project photo and you may discover a flurry of design concepts that might tickle your fancy. Homeowners can use this book as their very own kitchen design resource library, showing the artful photos to their selected design professional to more effectively communicate their preferences.

Kitchens are the most expensive room in the house to either equip or remodel. Anyone undertaking such a costly project wants to be assured of getting it right … of receiving a good value for the investment made.

This book does a great job of helping homeowners to get it right!

— Kenneth W. Peterson, CKD
President and founder of SEN Design Group, an organization of Kitchen and Bath professionals dedicated to providing the best investment value to their clients in both products and services.
www.sendesign.com

Introduction

Kitchens. The word itself brings up all sorts of visions – Mom at home; freshly baked cookies; hot coffee brewing on a cold morning; family discussions; a quick breakfast; homework projects; family pets; parties with friends; neighbors in for a chat....

Kitchens. The place where so much of our lives are spent on a daily basis: The heart of our homes.

Diana Farrell Serbe, Editor for inmamaskitchen. com, writes: "Keep that kitchen as beautiful as you can, for this is the room that promises to keep you together with your family and give you the center of nourishment, both for body and soul." We want our kitchen to be a reflection of ourselves, a comfortable and functional place. A place we like and are happy in. When those conditions are not met, it's time for a new kitchen!

With all that in mind, this pictorial guide contains design ideas to start those creative juices flowing. Most of these concepts can be used for any kitchen from budget to luxe, large or small with obvious space considerations observed.

In addition to being an idea generator, this guide will enable superior communication between the design professional and the consumer, for as we all know, "a picture is worth a thousand words." Seeing different ways of including a design element can help make selecting the best choice a lot easier. While each project is used to illustrate a certain design element, many other great design ideas might be present. In fact, many projects are loaded with wonderful ideas.

Included in the back of the book are the sources for the photographs that will allow the reader to obtain more information on any project pictured.

All of these photographs were taken by Steven Paul Whitsitt of Whitsitt Photography, with the permission of the designer and the homeowner. They come from all parts of the United States.

Photographer's Note

To me there is nothing more exciting than showing up at a home, walking in and finding a kitchen that is newly built or remodeled, and attempting to capture photographically the essence of what the designer and consumer envisioned. Each project presents its own unique set of challenges. I want to take just a moment to talk about my approach and techniques.

First, I shoot all of the images with a 4x5 view camera on Fuji color transparency film. I know that digital is rapidly replacing film, and I get asked pretty frequently why I still shoot on film. The short answer is that I feel that for image sharpness, accurate color representation, tonal range, and permanence, 4x5 is still superior to the best digital capture systems.

Most kitchens look perfectly illuminated with the lights that the designer or electrician provided. When making a photograph, the existing lighting is inadequate to evenly illuminate the entire room. To augment the existing light I use studio flashes with umbrellas or bounced off the ceiling to light the room. I try my best to balance the inside light with the outside, as I think that this gives the most natural representation

I use props to bring warmth and comfort to the photo. My idea is that I want the photo to look as if the homeowner was working in the kitchen and just stepped away for a moment to answer the door. Prop placement is often a collaborative effort between me, the designer, my wife, and, occasionally, the homeowner. This collaboration is frequently the most interesting part of a shoot, because it gives everyone the opportunity to have some input.

Finally, I absolutely insist on having fun. The work is hard, and sometimes stressful, but the schedule is never too tight to allow for an interesting conversation with a designer or homeowner about any topic under the sun. I sincerely hope that the joy that I experience in life and in doing my job is somehow captured in the images that I create.

SECTION I
Architectural Elements

We start our journey into the world of kitchen design by looking at the space setting. The overall space dimensions, the size and number of windows, the incorporation of columns or beams, and other structural elements impact our choices. Many of these elements we cannot change for they are integral to the overall structure as a part of the architecture of the home. Other times we can add, delete or alter these elements. Flooring and lighting selections greatly influence other choices in our kitchens. In any event, all of the architectural elements play a significant role in the final project. Let's look more closely at some of these elements.

Photo courtesy of A Kitchen & Bath Company, Millersville, MD

Chapter 1
Beams

The size, type, and color of the beams help set the style of the room. They can be natural logs, hewn timbers, rough-cut lumber, or man-made box beams, with or without interior moldings. They can be purely decorative or a structural necessity.

Photo courtesy of Kennedy Kitchen Distributors, Springfield, IL

An example of hewn beams used for decoration. *Photo courtesy of Black Diamond Kitchens, Inc., Fraser, CO*

Exposed 2x6 roof trusses are primarily structural, with a decorative effect secondary. *Photo courtesy of Spacial Design, San Anselmo, CA*

The dark stained exposed beams are structural. *Photo courtesy of Nordic Kitchens & Baths, Metaire, LA*

The light stained exposed beams are structural and the color echoes the woodwork.
Photo courtesy of Whole House Cabinetry, Glenmoore, PA

The beams are made of rough cut timber. *Photo courtesy of Country Cabinets, Etc., North Conway, NH*

Dark stained beams are used for decoration. *Photo courtesy of Columbine Kitchen & Bath, Castlerock, CO*

Manmade stained wood box beams are used for appearance. *Photo courtesy of Living Spaces Cabinet Design Studio, Hillsborough, NC*

These are a combination of hewn beam and rough cut manmade beams.
Photo courtesy of L & S Interiors, Anaheim, CA

Painted manmade box beams with additional moldings make
a formal look. *Photo courtesy of Bytner Design Associates,
Clarkson, MI*

Painted manmade very formal box beam construction has cross
members and elaborate detail. *Photo courtesy of Bella Domicile,
Madison, WI, and Brown House Designs, Madison, WI*

Chapter 2

Ceiling Treatments

In addition to having beams as a possible ceiling treatment, many other effects can impact the over all style of the kitchen project. Barrel ceilings, lowered ceilings, soffits, and tray ceilings are some architectural choices. In addition, there are a variety of different materials to choose from. They include painted sheetrock, natural or stained wood, blown ceilings, and tin ceiling tiles.

Photo courtesy of Kitchen Works, West Granby, CT

This kitchen sports a stained wood central barrel ceiling with soffit sides of standard construction. *Photo courtesy of Country Cabinets, Etc., North Conway, NH*

A complete barrel ceiling covers the entire kitchen space. The trim is painted wood. *Photo courtesy of Bytner Design Associates, Clarkson, MI*

An elaborate lowered ceiling defines the kitchen. Notice the edge detail, and the space next to the windows. *Photo courtesy of DCI Home Resource, Charlotte, NC*

Another example of a lowered soffit, in this case sometimes called a light bridge, because it has open areas. It defines the kitchen area within a larger space. *Photo courtesy of Wood-Stock Kitchens, Essex Junction, VT*

A large recess with a sky-light dominates the ceiling in this kitchen. *Photo courtesy of The Home Improvements Group, Woodland, CA*

The large center recess has a large molding detail inside the recess. *Photo courtesy of Kitchens By Teipen, Greenwood, IN*

A tin ceiling is an effective style statement. *Photo courtesy of Interstate Custom Kitchen & Bath, Inc., Chicopee, MA*

A wood ceiling brings the ceiling down and makes an intimate space. *Photo courtesy of Interstate Custom Kitchen & Bath, Inc., Chicopee, MA*

Chapter 3
Columns

The use of columns can be structural or ornamental or both. Columns can be used to define the kitchen space, separating it from the surrounding areas, or they can be used within the space for special effects. They are especially useful when adding on to the original kitchen space, as a decorative way of supporting the existing overhead structure.

Photo courtesy of Mary Laborde Interior Design, St. Simons Island, GA

The Doric-order columns are used to define the space and are purely ornamental. *Photo courtesy of Northbay Kitchen, Petaluma, CA*

A more elaborate and very formal use of Doric-order columns, faux painted to look like marble, defines the kitchen space. *Photo courtesy of Kitchen Gallery of Spring Grove, Spring Grove, IL*

These craftsman style columns are both functional and ornamental. *Photo courtesy of Kitchens By Teipen, Greenwood, IN*

Boxed columns separate and define the kitchen. In addition, they echo the architectural details of the adjoining rooms. *Photo courtesy of Kitchens By Teipen, Greenwood, IN*

These columns are supportive and decorative, in addition to being functional. *Photo courtesy of Kitchens By Teipen, Greenwood, IN*

An example of an expanded kitchen space where the left column is structural. The right column is purely ornamental. *Photo courtesy of Living Spaces Cabinetry Design Studio, Hillsborough, NC*

A boxed support column with details to complement the kitchen. *Photo courtesy of Bel Air Construction. Inc., Forest Hill, MD*

These columns are both structural and ornamental. *Photo courtesy of Northbay Kitchen, Petaluma, CA*

Chapter 4
Windows

Everyone loves a bright and airy kitchen. Windows, and lots of them, are seen as the primary way of accomplishing just that. Skylights, window walls, and focal point windows are a few ways that windows can be used. The following are some examples of each type.

Photo courtesy of T Squared Studios, Lafayette, CO

Skylights and windows between the countertop and wall cabinets provide natural lighting in this kitchen. *Photo courtesy of J.B. Turner & Sons, Oakland, CA*

A large skylight and larger windows between the countertop and the shortened wall cabinets provide the natural light for this kitchen. *Photo courtesy of Kitchens & Baths, Linda Burkhardt, Monatuk, NY*

Small skylights and a small wall of windows help light this kitchen. *Photo courtesy of Whole House Cabinetry, Inc., Glenmoore, PA*

Skylights and a large Palladian window provide light as well as a focal point for the kitchen. *Photo courtesy of The Kitchen Guide, Inc., Barrington, IL*

Arched windows provide focal points and natural light. *Photo courtesy of A Kitchen & Bath Company, Millersville, MD*

An eyebrow window over standard windows is used as a focal point. *Photo courtesy of The Cabinet Works, Stratham, NH*

Large window walls on two sides and cabinets with glass doors echo the windows. *Photo courtesy of Living Spaces Custom Design, Hillsborough, NC*

Continuous windows cover two walls providing lots of light and great views. *Photo courtesy of Classic Kitchen and Bath, Roslyn, NY*

An angled corner window has a corner sink below. *Photo courtesy of Roomscapes, Laguna Niguel, CA*

Square corner windows have an angled sink in front. *Photo courtesy of F&W Kitchens & Baths, Palm Desert, CA*

Chapter 5

Flooring

Photo courtesy of Kitchen Gallery of Spring Grove, Spring Grove, IL

Flooring is the foundation of the architectural space of our kitchens. Because it is one of the most used (and abused) surfaces, special consideration needs to be taken when making a selection, so that, over time, it will remain beautiful and functional. Fortunately, we have a variety of floor materials and finishes which help us keep the floors in great physical condition. In today's kitchens, wood and ceramic tile are the most common choices. Wood flooring may be prefinished, or finished on the job with a variety of finishes. Ceramic tiles come in many sizes and shapes. They come glazed and un-glazed. Glazed tile consists of a base material and a surface glaze baked on. Unglazed tile, such as porcelain, has the color constant through the thickness of the tile. The following examples show how the floor choice makes an impact in the kitchen design.

A wood floor in medium stain installed on the diagonal creates movement. *Photo courtesy of R & R Remodelers, Inc., Clifton, NJ*

A light wood floor is the same color as the cabinets. The darker inlay breaks up the cocoon effect of all wood in the same color tones. *Photo courtesy of Northbay Kitchen, Petaluma, CA*

A medium stained wood floor has both perimeter inlays and interior inlays.
Photo courtesy of The Home Improvement Group, Woodland, CA

A kitchen with a large black and white checkerboard floor makes a very traditional style. *Photo courtesy of Blau Bath & Kitchen, Milwaukee, WI*

This kitchen has a traditional small black and white checkerboard floor. *Photo courtesy of Rehm-Brandt's Design, Bennington, VT*

A variation of the checkerboard style has four large tiles surrounding a small tile. *Photo courtesy of T-Squared Studios, Lafayette, CO*

A ceramic tile floor with tile inlays creates a repeating square effect. It is laid on the diagonal to create movement. *Photo courtesy of Classic Kitchen & Bath, Roslyn, NY*

A ceramic tile floor with an inlaid medallion, creating a focal point in front of the range. *Photo courtesy of Interstate Custom Kitchen & Bath, Inc., Chicopee, MA*

A ceramic floor is laid in subway tile fashion. *Photo courtesy of Mark Klevan Cabinetry, Stamford, CT*

A large square tile floor laid on the diagonal with smaller tiles inserted around the island in a pattern forming a "rug." *Photo courtesy of Kitchens By Teipen, Greenwood, IN*

The large slate tile is laid on the diagonal. *Photo courtesy of Better Kitchen & Baths, Ventura, CA*

Chapter 6

Lighting

The inclusion of natural light has been covered in Chapter 4 on Windows. However, since most of us live in the contiguous forty-eight states of the United States, we need to address artificial lighting sources for that almost half of the year when our kitchens are dark in the morning and in the late afternoon/evening. Popular choices today include recess can lights for general lighting, under cabinet lights to light the work surfaces, and task lighting for the cooking, clean-up, and eating spaces. All lighting affects the ambiance of the space, while some adds significantly to the style of the kitchen.

Photo courtesy of Coastal Kitchen & Bath Design, York, ME

Two central lights work well for a small kitchen. *Photo courtesy of Blossom Brothers, Inc., Delray Beach, FL*

A central fixture in a recess with a few recessed lights for task lighting over the sink is all that's needed. *Photo courtesy of Spacial Design, San Anselmo, CA*

A combination of recessed lights, a central fixture, and a pendant light offers plenty of light. *Photo courtesy of Callen Construction, Muskego, WI*

A combination of recessed lights and two pendants over the eating area lights this space. *Photo courtesy of Wood-Stock Kitchens, Essex Junction, VT*

The lighting for this space is a combination of recessed lights and pendants over the island. *Photo courtesy of Bella Domicile, Madison, WI*

A combination of recessed lights and a chandelier over the island gives a traditional look. *Photo courtesy of DCI Home Resource, Charlotte, NC*

A combination of recessed lights, a pendant over the island, and wall sconces over the eating area lights this kitchen. *Photo courtesy of Bel Air Construction, Inc., Forest Hill, MD*

A fan light as central lighting, with recessed lights for darker areas, provides air circulation as well as lighting. *Photo courtesy of City Kitchens, Cambridge, MA*

This kitchen has fan lights, and track lighting around the skylights. *Photo courtesy of Charlestowne Kitchen & Bath, St Charles, IL*

Right:
Track lighting is all that is needed for this compact kitchen. *Photo courtesy of Solara Designs, Williston Park, NY*

Far right:
Suspended track lighting around the perimeter of the kitchen is featured here. *Photo courtesy of Spacial Design, San Anselmo, CA*

Small lights above every cabinet door offer lighting for both outside and inside the cabinets. *Photo courtesy of DCI Home Resource, Charlotte, NC*

SECTION II
Elements of the Work Space

The elements that are included/excluded from the working areas greatly impact the functionality of the kitchen. Many people think that once the sink, range, and refrigerator are placed, the kitchen is designed. The reality is that these elements, while important, are only part of the overall design. Other elements such as ovens, microwaves, and islands also have an impact on functionality with a lesser impact on esthetics. Correct placement of these elements, with the necessary supporting cabinetry, is challenging and needs expertise. Let's look at some of the elements needed for a great working kitchen.

Photo courtesy of Lemont Kitchens & Baths, Lemont, IL

Chapter 7
The Wet Center
Sinks and Dishwashers

One of the hardest working elements in the kitchen is today's kitchen sink. We currently have many configurations to choose from and many choices among materials. The current most common choice is a stainless steel sink, chosen for its beauty and durability. Putting a sink together with a dishwasher, you now have the key parts needed for food preparation and clean up. The following are some examples of sink-dishwasher combinations. Whether they are placed in a corner, under a window or on an island, their primary functions remain the same. Let's take a look at some of today's options.

Photo courtesy of Coastal Kitchen & Bath Designs, York, ME

This kitchen has a black two bowl sink under a window with a black dishwasher. *Photo courtesy of Northbay Kitchen, Petaluma, CA*

A stainless steel large bowl and smaller bowl sink is under a window with a two drawer dishwasher with wood panel fronts. *Photo courtesy of The Kitchen Guide, Inc., Barrington, IL*

A stainless steel sink with two equal bowls is in a corner installation with a foot pedal to control the water. A full height wood panel completely disguises the dishwasher. *Photo courtesy of Kitchen Concepts, Inc., Cincinnati, OH*

A single bowl stainless steel sink in a corner setting under a window has a full height wood panel front for the dishwasher. *Photo courtesy of Kitchen Classics by Custom Crafters, Arlington, VA*

A two equal bowl stainless steel sink with hutch-like cabinetry above, against a wall provides a focal point, has a full height wood panel dishwasher nearby. *Photo courtesy of Kitchens By Teipen, Greenwood, IN*

A single bowl farmhouse sink in porcelain under a window is featured with a white dishwasher. *Photo courtesy of Custom Crafters, Kensington, MD*

A large bowl, small bowl stainless steel sink with integral drain board and a two drawer dishwasher with wood panel fronts are set against a wall with cabinets above. *Photo courtesy of Lindquist and Co., Duluth, MN*

43

A large single bowl stainless steel farmhouse sink is featured with a single drawer stainless steel dishwasher. *Photo courtesy of Architectural Kitchenworks, Schrewsbury, NJ*

A very large copper farmhouse sink is shown with a panel clad black trimmed dishwasher. *Photo courtesy of Kitchen & Bath Design Studio, Div. Of Wagner Fabrication, West Salem, WI*

A copper single sink with copper drain boards is on an island. *Photo courtesy of Kitchens, Etc., Framingham, MA*

A raised dishwasher with full cabinetry panel is on the far left of this island, with landing space next to the double bowl sink. *Photo courtesy of Kitchen Gallery, Knoxville, TN*

A round single stainless steel bowl is on an island with a single drawer stainless dishwasher. *Photo courtesy of Trubilt Home Products, Paterson, NJ*

Chapter 8
The Hot Center:
Ranges and Cooktops

Cooking over open flames has been a part of food preparation since humanity discovered fire. The cooking center has gone through considerable evolution since then. First, it went to an outside cook house with a large fireplace and then inside to a hearth room with a cooking fireplace and ovens. Today, we see vestiges of parts of the evolutionary process. We have cooking centers in hearth-like settings and we still cook with open flames (gas). We also have cooking centers that have evolved far beyond fires. We have smooth-top cooktops and downdraft ventilation. Regardless of the style and the source of heat, the cooking center is a major part of a working kitchen.

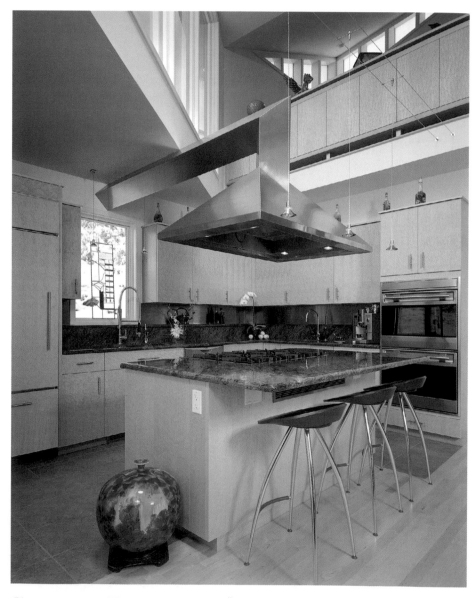

Photo courtesy of T-Squared Studios, Lafayette, CO

Photo courtesy of Kitchens Unlimited, Memphis, TN

A hearth style center has cabinets inside the stone surround and a gas range. *Photo courtesy of Jan Merrell Kitchens, Toledo, OH*

A hearth style hot center has a stone surround and a gas range. *Photo courtesy of Blossom Brothers, Inc., Del Ray Beach, FL*

A hearth style hot center has a partial brick surround and a gas range. *Photo courtesy of Bella Domicile, Madison, WI*

A hearth style center has a separate gas cook top and oven. Cabinets pull out and are topped by a mantle. *Photo courtesy of Builder Specialties, Montpelier, VT*

A hearth style center has a gas cooktop, pot filler, and cabinet surround. Cabinets have storage on open shelves, accessed from within the hearth area with a mantle above. *Photo courtesy of Coastal Kitchen & Bath Designs, York, ME*

A hearth style center has a gas range, a wall mounted utensil rack, and open shelves behind the surrounding cabinetry with mantle above. *Photo courtesy of Roomscapes, Laguna Niguel, CA*

A modified hearth style center has a reproduction vintage gas range and no surround or mantle. *Photo courtesy of Kitchen Concepts of Durango, Durango, CO*

A hearth style center has a gas range, slender cabinets on sides that have storage inside, and a mantle. *Photo courtesy of Custom Crafters, Inc., Kensington, MD*

A modified hearth style center has an electric smooth top cooktop, separate oven, and separate grill under a modified hearth with a mantle and no surround. *Photo courtesy of Mark Klevan Cabinetry, Stamford, CT*

The large hood over a gas range serves as a focal point for the room. *Photo courtesy of DCI Home Resource, Charlotte, NC*

This hot center has a gas range and large hood. Elaborate corbels below hood, moldings and onlays above, in addition to a contrasting color, make a strong focal point. *Photo courtesy of R & R Remodelers, Inc., Clifton, NJ*

A dramatic hot center has a gas range, large hood, and large opening to the dining area. *Photo courtesy of The Kitchen Guide, Inc., Barrington, IL*

A hot center has a gas range under a round front stainless steel hood. *Photo courtesy of Custom Crafters Inc., Kensington, MD*

A hot center has a gas range and a rectangular stainless steel hood. *Photo courtesy of DCI Home Resource, Charlotte, NC*

The hood is behind cabinetry. The gas cooktop and separate oven are below. *Photo courtesy of The Kitchen Source, San Francisco, CA*

The hot center has a gas cooktop and combination stainless and glass hood. *Photo courtesy of Kitchens By Weiland, Allentown, PA*

A hot center has a gas cooktop, separate oven, and round front stainless steel hood. *Photo courtesy of Kitchens and Baths, Linda Butkhardt, Montauk, NY*

A gas cooktop, stainless steel hood, and stainless steel wall/backsplash make for the hot center. *Photo courtesy of Jan Merrell Kitchens, Toledo, OH*

A hot center on an island has a gas cooktop and stainless steel hood. *Photo courtesy of Shelly Design, Cincinnati, OH*

The peninsula has an electric smooth top cooktop and stainless steel hood in its hot center. *Photo courtesy of Washtenaw Woodwrights, Inc., Ann Arbor, MI*

A hot center on an island has an integral electric glass smooth top cooktop in a granite countertop. *Photo courtesy Thomas Lewis & Co., Lyons, CO*

The hot center on an island has a gas cooktop and downdraft ventilation system. *Photo courtesy of Whole House Cabinetry, Inc., Glenmoore, PA*

A hot center on an island has an gas cooktop and downdraft ventilation. *Photo courtesy of The Kitchen Guide, Inc., Barrington, IL*

This hot center has a microwave over a separate gas cooktop and oven. *Photo courtesy of A Kitchen & Bath Company, Millersville, MD*

Chapter 9

The Cold Center:
Refrigerators and Freezers

The cold center is the third major area of the work space. We have full door refrigerators and freezers; refrigerators with freezers on the top, on the side or on the bottom; refrigerators or freezers in drawers as separate units or as part of a complete unit. Let's look at some of these and how they are included in the kitchen to stand out or blend in so that they disappear.

Photo courtesy of The Cabinetworks, Stratham, NH

The refrigerator almost disappears into the cabinetry. *Photo courtesy of DCI Home Resource, Charlotte, NC*

A single door stainless refrigerator has two freezer drawers adjacent, with cabinetry fronts. *Photo courtesy of DCI Home Resource, Charlotte, NC*

A side by side refrigerator/freezer has ice and water through the door. *Photo courtesy of All Trades Contracting, Inc., Clinton, NJ*

Two full door units, refrigerator and freezer, have a stainless steel finish. *Photo courtesy of Appliance Associates of Buffalo, Buffalo, NY*

A top mount freezer, with a refrigerator below, has a deep cabinet above and no side panel. *Photo courtesy of Builders Specialties, Montpelier, VT*

A reproduction bottom mount freezer, refrigerator above has a cabinet surround with a decorative open space including a bead board back over the refrigerator. *Photo courtesy of Kitchens Concepts of Durango, Durango, CO*

Stainless steel full door freezer and a glass fronted full door refrigerator are side by side with open decorative spaces above. *Photo courtesy of Trubilt Home Products, Inc., Paterson, NJ*

Glass fronted full door refrigerator has painted trim, cabinetry surround. *Photo courtesy of Kitchen Works, West Granby, CT*

Side by side refrigerator/freezer has wood panel fronts, and a cabinet surround. *Photo courtesy of DMR Remodeling, Inc., Park Hills, KY*

Side by side refrigerator/freezer has painted wood panel fronts and cabinet surround. *Photo courtesy of Southern Kitchens, Inc., Alexandria, VA*

Side by side refrigerator freezer has ice and water through the door with wood panel fronts and a cabinet surround. *Photo courtesy of Intercoastal Kitchen & Bath, Naples, FL*

Side by side refrigerator/freezer has wood panel fronts, and cabinetry designed to look like a free standing piece of furniture. *Photo courtesy of Black Diamond Kitchens, Inc., Fraser, CO*

Chapter 10

Microwaves

Microwaves are an important part of any kitchen today. They are usually part of either the hot center or the cold center. The microwave oven cooks by agitating the water and\or fat molecules in the food. They do not brown the food, so cakes or chickens microwaved come out looking pale and unappetiz-ing. The microconvection oven does brown the food, but the texture is not the same as food roasted in a dry oven. Nevertheless, a microwave is a must for almost every kitchen. There are numerous ways they can be included.

Photo courtesy of Kitchens By Teipen, Greenwood, CO

A microwave is near the refrigerator under a wall cabinet with no shelf below. *Photo courtesy of Coastal Kitchen & Bath Designs, York, ME*

This microwave built into a wall cabinet near the refrigerator has an open shelf above. *Photo courtesy of Modern Kitchen & Bath, Troy, MI*

The microwave is built into a deep wall cabinet with a wood surround. *Photo courtesy Detailed Builders, Inc., Palatine, IL*

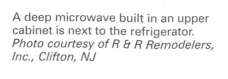

A deep microwave built in an upper cabinet is next to the refrigerator. *Photo courtesy of R & R Remodelers, Inc., Clifton, NJ*

The microwave is hidden behind a flip up door next to the refrigerator.
Photo courtesy of DCI Home Resource, Charlotte, NC

A deep microwave is built-in under a deep wall cabinet just above the countertop.
Photo courtesy of Appliance Associates of Buffalo, Buffalo, NY

A microwave is on a shelf over an appliance garage and under a wall cabinet.
Photo courtesy of Kitchen Works, West Granby, CT

A microwave is on a shelf in a deep wall cabinet in the cold center.
Photo courtesy of Terra Nova Kitchen & Bath, Vienna, VA

A microwave is built-in over an appliance garage under a wall cabinet next to the refrigerator. *Photo courtesy of Gilman Screens & Kitchens, San Francisco, CA*

A microwave is on the lowered counter, easily accessible by someone in a wheelchair. *Photo courtesy of Callen Construction, Muskeego, WI*

A built-in corner microwave is under a TV. *Photo courtesy of Kitchens Unlimited, Memphis, TN*

An under counter built-in microwave is in an island. *Photo courtesy of Trubilt Home Products, Inc., Paterson, NJ*

An under counter built-in microwave is in the hot center. *Photo courtesy of The Home Improvements Group, Woodland, CA*

A built-in under counter microwave is part of the hot center. *Photo courtesy of Charlestowne Kitchen & Bath, St. Charles, IL*

The built-in under counter microwave is in a raised portion of an island. *Photo courtesy of Low Country Kitchen & Bath, Hilton Head Island, SC*

A microwave is over a built-in range. *Photo courtesy of The Kitchen Guide, Inc., Barrington, IL*

The microwave is over the cooktop. *Photo courtesy of Homewood Kitchen & Bath, Inc., Homewood, IL*

Every kitchen needs an oven or ovens. Microwave ovens were covered in Chapter 10. In this chapter we look at different ways that a thermal or convection oven or ovens can be included. Food in a thermal oven is heated by the natural flow of air created when hot air rises and cooler air falls around the food. In a convection oven, a fan in the oven cavity continually circulates the hot air so that the food is constantly bathed in hot air. Ovens that are separate from the cooktop do not have to be in the hot center. Ranges that have the oven or ovens under the cooktop were shown in Chapter 8.

Photo courtesy of Living Spaces Cabinet Design Studio, Batavia, OH

A single oven is in the end of an island. *Photo courtesy of Kitchen Works, West Granby, CT*

A single oven over a warming drawer is in a tall cabinet. *Photo courtesy of Kitchen Works, West Granby, CT*

Black glass double ovens are in a tall cabinet. *Photo courtesy of Mark Klevan Cabinetry, Stamford, CT*

Two stainless single ovens are under an island countertop. *Photo courtesy of The Kitchen Guide, Inc., Barrington, IL*

A primary oven as part of the range is in the hot center. A second stainless oven is under a microwave in a wall. *Photo courtesy of Homewood Kitchen & Bath, Homewood, IL*

A range with one oven and a second oven is part of the island. *Photo Courtesy of The Cabinet Works, Stratham, NH*

Single stainless steel oven under a microwave and over a warming drawer is in a tall cabinet. *Photo courtesy of Kitchen Concepts, Cincinnati, OH*

Double black ovens are built into a corner wall. *Photo courtesy of Kitchen & Bath Design Studio, div of Wagner Fabrication, West Salem, WI*

Double ovens, over and under, are part of a range. *Photo courtesy of Country Cupboards, Kingston, NY*

Chapter 12
Island Configurations

Islands come in every imaginable size and shape: some are small, some are huge. They can be one level or multi-leveled. Most make a kitchen more efficient and help direct traffic away from the preparation, cooking, and clean-up areas. Many islands also have an eating space for snacks or quick meals. These snack spaces can be at table height, counter height or bar height. The following are examples of each type.

Photo courtesy of The Cabinet Works, Stratham, NH

A T-shaped island has a prep sink. *Photo courtesy of Classic Kitchen & Bath, Roslyn, NY*

A single level island has a curved knee space at counter height. *Photo courtesy of Living Spaces Cabinet Design Studio, Batavia, OH*

An irregularly shaped island has cooktop and sink close together. *Photo courtesy of Better Kitchens & Baths, Ventura, CA*

A large, basically rectangular island has a shaped countertop. *Photo courtesy of Lifestyle Kitchen & Bath Center, Parker, CO*

A large single level island is almost square and has a snack space at counter height. *Photo courtesy of Trubilt Home Products, Inc., Paterson, NJ*

A single level island has a prep sink at one end and an under counter refrigerator/ wine storage at the other. *Photo courtesy of Prescott Stone Fabricators, Durham, NC*

A single level rectangular island has a large overhang eating area. *Photo courtesy of Kitchen Concepts, Inc., Cincinnati, OH*

A multi-shaped island with a prep sink at one end, cook top on the other, and counter height attached eating space. *Photo courtesy of Black Diamond Kitchens, Inc., Fraser, CO*

A rectangular island has multi-levels and a cooktop. *Photo courtesy of The Kitchen Guide, Inc., Barrington, IL*

A rectangular island has prep sink, large cooktop, and bar height snack space. *Photo courtesy of Artisan Kitchen & Bath, San Jose, CA*

A two level island has a prep sink and a table height snack space. *Photo courtesy of Architectural Kitchenworks, Schrewsbury, NJ*

Two level island has a large angular bar height snack space. *Photo courtesy of Trubilt Home Products, Inc., Paterson, NJ*

A multi-level island has a prep sink and counter height snack space on three sides. *Photo courtesy of Whole House Cabinetry, Inc., Glenmoore, PA*

A multi-level island has a primary sink, dishwasher, garbage disposal, and bar height snack space. *Photo courtesy of Kitchens By Teipen, Greenwood, IN*

The two sides of the multi-level island has a curved eating space, prep sink, and professional style cook top. *Photo courtesy of Kuntriset Kitchens, Norwich, NY*

Two level island has a large curved bar height snack space. *Photo courtesy of Country Cabinets, Etc., North Conway, NH*

Two small islands have sinks, one with eating space at counter height. *Photo courtesy of Atlantic Coast Kitchen & Bath of Jacksonville, Orange Park, FL*

Two islands, one has a sink and the other has raised storage. *Photo courtesy of The Home Improvements Group, Woodland, CA*

The two islands are connected by a removable bridge that serves as a bar height snack space. *Photo courtesy of DCI Home Resource, Charlotte, NC*

Two islands: one has a farm sink, the other has snack space. *Photo courtesy of Atwood: Fine Architectural Cabinetry, Birmingham, MI*

Two islands, one has an apron front prep sink and one has counter height snack space. *Photo courtesy of Cassedy & Fahrbach, Pittsboro, NC*

The "U" shaped kitchen has a big island in the center. *Photo courtesy of The Cabinet Tree, Germantown, TN*

A large multi-purpose island connected to the ceiling lends privacy to the work centers and serves as eating and desk space in addition to adding lots of storage. *Photo courtesy of The Cabinet Tree, Germantown, TN*

SECTION III
Detail Elements

The detail elements of a kitchen greatly enrich the appearance, while having a lesser impact upon the functionality of the kitchen. The selection of these elements, and how they are incorporated, makes each kitchen "special." All of the concepts presented on the following pages require some expertise to make the project have a "correct" feel. Following the design principles of balance, rhythm, emphasis, and repetition takes knowledge and practice. On the following pages are some great examples.

Photo courtesy of Bella Domicile, Madison, WI

Chapter 13
Stacked Cabinets

When the walls are very high, stacking cabinets can give added storage while keeping everything in proportion. Stacking cabinets also allow for floor to ceiling cabinetry, a very useful technique for small kitchens, where every inch counts. Stacking cabinets mean literally piling one cabinet upon another. When this is done, the seam where the two cabinets come together is visible and not considered attractive. To hide this seam, some designers use exterior panels applied over the sides of the cabinet and others design in an appropriate molding detail. The following are some examples of stacked cabinets, showing how the space is efficiently used.

Photo courtesy of Kitchen Gallery of Spring Grove, Spring Grove, IL

Glass door cabinets are stacked on regular height cabinets. *Photo courtesy of Wellesley Kitchens, Inc., Welesley, MA*

Stacked cabinets with a combination of open, closed, and glass doors keeps the cabinetry in proportion to the height of the space. *Photo courtesy of Bella Domicile, Madison, WI*

Both closed and glass door cabinets are used here. *Photo courtesy of Classic Kitchen & Bath, Roslyn, NY*

Glass door cabinets stacked on the closed door lower cabinets echo the pattern of the kitchen window. *Photo courtesy of Atwood: Fine Architectural Cabinetry, Birmingham, MI*

A row of glass door cabinets stacked above closed door cabinets go floor to ceiling. *Photo courtesy of Shelly Design, Inc., Cincinnati, OH*

Tall cabinets with glass doors over glass or closed doors give a stacked look for spaces with lower ceilings. *Photo courtesy of Expressions Kitchen & Bath Design Studio, Sudbury, MA*

Tall cabinets with glass doors above solid doors give a stacked cabinet look.
Photo courtesy of Kitchen Concepts, Inc., Cincinnati, OH

Tall cabinets with two panels gives the look of stacked cabinets. *Photo courtesy of Wood-Stock Kitchens, Essex Junction, VT*

Stacked cabinets go floor to ceiling. *Photo courtesy of Gilman Screens & Kitchens, San Francisco, CA*

Stacked cabinets go floor to ceiling in a small kitchen. *Photo courtesy of T-Squared Studios, Lafayette, CO*

Chapter 14

Multi-height Cabinets

One way to add visual interest to a wall of cabinets is to stagger the height of those cabinets. There are a number of ways in which this concept may be used. Here are a few examples of different ways that multi-height cabinets can add interest to the kitchen.

Photo courtesy of Kitchens By Teipen, Greenwood, IN

This kitchen has taller cabinets that serve as focal points. *Photo courtesy of Roomscapes, Laguna Niguel, CA*

Varied height cabinets add interest to this kitchen. *Photo courtesy of Appliance Associates of Buffalo, Buffalo, NY*

The stepped height of the wall cabinets echoes and emphasizes the ceiling line. *Photo Courtesy of Carmike Kitchens, Mechanicsville, MD*

Varied height cabinets allow for display space in this kitchen. *Photo courtesy of Bella Domicile, Madison, NY*

The varied heights give richness of detail to this contemporary kitchen. *Photo Courtesy of Cabinet Source, Biloxi, MS*

These staggered height cabinets add storage and interest. *Photo courtesy of Bella Domicile, Madison, WI*

The taller cabinets provide focal points and have arched door tops echoing the kitchen window. *Photo courtesy of Custom Design, Oakhurst, CA*

Chapter 15
Multi-colored Cabinets

A different approach to making a kitchen more interesting is to use more than one color for the cabinetry and/or trims. It takes an experienced design professional to do this successfully. The following are some exciting and wonderful kitchens using more than one color.

Photo courtesy of Bertch Custom Cabinetry, Waterloo, IA, and Appliance Associates of Buffalo, Buffalo, NY

This kitchen has perimeter cabinets of white, and black cabinets for the island.
Photo courtesy of Cederberg Kitchens and Additions, Chapel Hill, NC

Medium stained cabinets for the perimeter cabinets and white for the island cabinets creates a two-toned kitchen. *Photo courtesy of The Cabinetworks, Stratham, NH*

The blue island cabinets are echoed in the backsplash color and again in the chair seats and rug, while the main perimeter cabinets are a light gray. *Photo courtesy of Wellseley Kitchens, Inc., Wellesley, MA*

Medium stain for the perimeter cabinets and distressed black for the island, creates a two-toned look. *Photo courtesy of The Kitchen Guide, Inc., Barrington, IL*

This kitchen has basic white cabinets with many touches of stained cabinets.
Photo courtesy of Kuntriset Kitchens, Norwich, NY

Dark cabinets and a white island with a white hood creates a different two-toned look.
Photo courtesy of Shelly Design, Inc Cincinnati, OH

Blocks of color provide another way to create a two-toned kitchen: A block around the sink, another around the range, and a third on the island. *Photo courtesy of Trubuilt Home Products Inc, Paterson, NJ*

This kitchen has three colors for its cabinetry. *Photo courtesy of Country Cupboards, Kingston, NY*

The colorful painted cabinets of the hot center pops out of this kitchen and gives lots of punch. *Photo courtesy of Carmike Kitchens, Mechanicsville, MD*

This kitchen has cabinetry in three colors. *Photo courtesy of Southern Kitchens Inc., Alexandria, VA*

A block of cabinets around the sink and a block of color on the island create interest in this two-toned kitchen. *Photo courtesy of The Cabinet Works, Stratham, NH*

A white island and hood in a kitchen of dark cabinets gives a strong two-toned look. *Photo courtesy of Bella Domicile, Madison, WI*

Blocks of color create the design theme for this kitchen. *Photo courtesy The Kitchen Source, San Francisco, CA*

White cabinets are on two sides of the kitchen and red cabinets on the other.
Photo courtesy of Spacial Design, San Anselmo, CA

Contrasting the light and dark colors of the cabinetry creates an exciting contemporary kitchen. *Photo courtesy of Bella Domicile, Madison, WI*

The base cabinet color is echoed as part of the trim, while the wall cabinets are a contrasting color. *Photo courtesy of City Kitchens, Cambridge, MA*

The two colors are used in the cabinets: a base color for the cabinet with a contrasting color for the doors and drawer fronts, and in the trims where a combination of the two colors are used. *Photo courtesy of Kitchen Gallery of Spring Grove, Spring Grove, IL*

Chapter 16

Multi-countertop Materials

Using a combination of materials for the countertops in today's kitchens not only creates visual excitement but different materials function in different ways. Wooden countertops are the easiest on sharp knives, thus making for excellent cutting spaces. The new treatment processes for these wood counters make them available for use just about anywhere. Granite is still the best surface for rolling pastry and is not affected by heat. It also grabs the viewer's attention. Soapstone is a natural stone product. It is non-porous, but it is easily scratched because it is so soft. Concrete is a material that is new to the countertop scene. Its greatest asset is that it can be formed into any shape. Ceramic tile provides a wide variety of patterns and colors and has been very popular in the West and Southwest for many years. Plastic laminates were invented in the late 1920s and have had wide use ever since. Once used as the most popular countertop material, they have fallen out of favor. They are still a good choice, since they are reasonably priced and offer a wide variety of colors and textures. Stainless steel is the most indestructible countertop material, and is the material of choice in commercial kitchens for its easy cleanability. Solid surface material, such as Corian, is a product made of plastics. It can be worked like wood, is easy to clean, and allows for integral sink installations. Engineered stone is made of quartz stone and acrylic plastics, offering the heat tolerance of stone with the ease of cleaning of a solid surface.

The island countertop is made of pyrolav, a unique and expensive (about twice granite) French product of lava stone that has been enameled and fired, while the other countertops are granite. *Photo courtesy of Kuche + Cucina, Paramus, NJ*

A combination of wood, concrete, and granite countertops is used in this kitchen. *Photo courtesy of The Home Improvements Group, Woodland, CA*

Wood and granite are combined very effectively. *Photo courtesy of Coastal Kitchen & Bath Designs, York, ME*

A combination of granite and wood using interesting shapes. *Photo courtesy of Black Diamond Kitchens, Inc., Fraser, CO*

Wood countertops are used on the island and granite on the perimeter cabinets. *Photo courtesy of Atlantic Coast Kitchen & Bath of Jacksonville, Orange Park, FL*

A wood countertop is on the island and a laminate with wood edge is on the "L" shaped cabinets. *Photo courtesy of Cederberg Kitchens & Additions, Chapel Hill, NC*

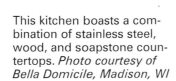

This kitchen boasts a combination of stainless steel, wood, and soapstone countertops. *Photo courtesy of Bella Domicile, Madison, WI*

Wood and two different color granites make the countertops in this kitchen.
Photo courtesy of Bella Domicile, Madison, WI

Ceramic tile is used for the major countertops and wood is used for the snack bar.
Photo courtesy of Northwoods Kitchens, Inc., Traverse City, MI

This kitchen has granite countertops for the main areas and has a wood snack bar.
Photo courtesy of Country Cabinets, etc, North Conway, NH

Corian and granite make an interesting combination of countertops.
Photo courtesy of Bella Domicile, Madison, WI

Two different granites are used for these countertops. *Photo courtesy of Northbay Kitchen, Petaluma, CA*

Granite is used for the perimeter cabinets and a combination of wood and glass is used on the island. *Photo courtesy of The Kitchen Source, San Francisco, CA*

The primary countertops are granite and copper is used for the raised portion of the island. *Photo courtesy of Kitchen Gallery, Knoxville, TN*

Chapter 17

Backsplashes

Backsplashes are that space between the countertop and the upper cabinets along the walls of a kitchen. The materials chosen to cover this area may be primarily functional or may be both functional and aesthetic. The areas behind the sink and the cooktop/range usually require special attention, because these areas get the most spattering and need frequent cleaning.

Photo courtesy of Country Cupboards, Kingston, NY

A full granite backsplash is used in this kitchen. *Photo courtesy of The Kitchen Guide, Inc., Barrington, IL*

This kitchen has a 4" granite backsplash and painted walls. *Photo courtesy of Coastal Kitchen & Bath Designs, York, ME*

Walls clad in colored tile, including the backsplash areas, makes a strong design statement. *Photo courtesy of Kitchens & Baths, Linda Burkhardt, Montauk, NY*

The backsplash and wall behind the cooktop are covered in diamond shaped tiles. *Photo courtesy of Kitchen Places, Ventura, CA*

A tile backsplash has a built-in niche above the cooktop. *Photo courtesy of J.B. Turner & Sons, Oakland, CA*

This kitchen has a 4" granite backsplash, painted walls, and tile behind the range.
Photo courtesy of Coastal Kitchen & Bath Design, York, ME

A full tile backsplash with tiles set on the diagonal has a deco panel insert above the range.
Photo courtesy of The Home Improvements Group, Woodland, CA

This full tile backsplash has a contrasting color deco inset over the range and small tile inserts echoing the floor design. *Photo courtesy of Roomscapes, Laguna Niguel, CA*

A tiled backsplash has deco tiles behind the range and along the other areas of the backsplash. *Photo courtesy of Kitchen Classics by Custom Crafters, Kensington, MD*

A full tile backsplash has a scenic deco in a tiled frame behind the cooktop and a tiled deco strip around the kitchen. *Photo courtesy of Classic Kitchen & Bath, Roslyn, NY*

A tiled backsplash has a stainless steel insert behind the range and glass block inserts.
Photo courtesy of The Home Improvements Group, Woodland, CA

Chapter 18

Top Trim

Top trim is one of those finishing details that needs to be addressed by the designer of the kitchen. The trim can be very simple or quite elaborate, depending on the style of the kitchen. Cabinets without top moldings often look unfinished. A wide variety of trims are shown in the following photos.

Photo courtesy of Finial Properties, Downers Grove, IL, and Lemont Kitchen & Bath, Lemont, IL

Shaker style cabinets have no top trim. *Photo courtesy of Bella Domicile, Madison, WI*

A kitchen that has a simple contrasting molding. *Photo courtesy of Mark Klevan Cabinetry, Stamford, CT*

This shaker kitchen has a simple looking top molding that continues over both the cooktop area and the sink area complete with small wood soffit that creates great continuity. *Photo courtesy of Classic Kitchen & Bath, Roslyn, NY*

A simple top trim completes this kitchen. *Photo courtesy of Classic Kitchen & Bath, Roslyn, NY*

A two-toned top trim gives added interest. *Photo courtesy of Washtenaw Woodwrights, Inc., Ann Arbor, MI*

The top trim here is layered, with curved edges that echo the doors of the cabinets. *Photo courtesy of The Kitchen Guide, Inc., Barrington, IL*

This kitchen has two separate trims: one around the entire space, and the other around the tops of the cabinets. *Photo courtesy of Bella Domicile, Madison, WI*

This kitchen has a layered top trim. *Photo courtesy of Blau Bath & Kitchen, Milwaukee, WI*

An elaborate layered top trim tops these cabinets. *Photo courtesy of Southern Kitchens, Alexandria, VA*

The soffit in this kitchen has molding above and a two-toned molding below. *Photo courtesy of L & S Interiors, Anaheim, CA*

The shaker kitchen has a soffit constructed of wood panels that match the cabinet doors.
Photo courtesy of Washtenaw Woodwrights Inc., Ann Arbor, MI

The kitchen has two higher pediments adding interest and richness to the basic design.
Photo courtesy of Lang's Kitchen & Bath, Newtown, PA

SECTION IV
Supplemental Elements

The supplemental elements, such as attached tables, built-in seating, pantries, and wine storage that we include here, answer specific needs. Attached tables are a great way to give a small kitchen much needed counter space and additional storage. While built-in seating can be incorporated and used in several ways, it usually adds great warmth and hominess, especially where space is limited. Pantries and wine storage spaces answer specific storage concerns while adding that touch of elegance often found in larger kitchens. Accessory cabinets provide additional storage and working spaces while using the same cabinetry for continuity.

Photo courtesy of Kitchens By Teipen, Greenwood, IN

Chapter 19
Attached Tables

Tables can be attached to a corner or a wall, attached to the back of cabinets, to a row of cabinets or to an island. In each case, they allow for a better functioning kitchen. Attached tables conserve space by eliminating one or more walkways. The attached tables can be at table height or counter height. Both heights offer more usable counter workspace as well as eating space.

Photo courtesy of Kitchen Classics by Custom Crafters, Arlington, VA

A small corner table for two gives eating space not otherwise possible in this kitchen. *Photo courtesy of Custom Crafters, Inc., Kensington, MD*

This table is attached to a wall with surrounding cabinets providing storage. *Photo courtesy of Kitchen & Bath Design Consultants, LLC, West Hartford, CT*

The table is attached to the back of some cabinets. *Photo courtesy of Classic Kitchen & Bath, Roslyn, NY*

A table is projected out from a wall. *Photo courtesy of Jan Merrell Kitchens, Toledo, OH*

An attached table is at the end of an island. *Photo courtesy of Lemont Kitchen & Bath, Lemont, IL*

An extended round table for four is at the end of an island. *Photo courtesy of Kitchen & Bath Galleries, Raleigh, NC*

The countertop is extended to form a table at the end of the island. *Photo courtesy of Northwoods Kitchens, Traverse City, MI*

The hexagonal table is attached to the island. *Photo courtesy of Detailed Builders Inc., Palatine, IL*

A raised table for four at the end of the island offers seating, in addition to the snack space at the back of the island. *Photo courtesy of L & S Interiors, Anaheim, CA*

An extended table attached to the island gives eating space for ten plus, some behind the sink area and some at the table end. *Photo courtesy of Kitchens Etc., Framingham, MA*

The wrap around counter is extended to form a table with cabinetry support at the end of the table. *Photo courtesy of Bella Domicile, Madison, WI*

Chapter 20

Built-in Seating

Built-in window seats have been a part of traditional architecture for many centuries. These seats add a cozy hominess to the kitchens they are used in. Other types of built-in seating, such as banquettes, may or may not be under windows. Banquettes that include built-in seating are a useful way of allowing for a table when space is limited. They are usually made of cabinetry parts, sometimes with storage under the seats, or materials that match the woodwork trim in the home. The following are some good examples.

Photo courtesy of Lang's Kitchen & Bath, Inc., Newtown, PA

The window seat gives continuity to the cabinetry. *Photo courtesy of Living Spaces Custom Design, Batavia, OH*

The window seat connects the two tall cabinets by the window. *Photo courtesy of Cederberg Kitchens & Additions, Chapel Hill, NC*

The window seat serves as additional seating for the table. *Photo courtesy of Kuntriset Kitchens, Norwich, NY*

This banquette has built-in seating on two sides, with extra seating provided by chairs. *Photo courtesy of Lindquist & Co., Duluth, MN*

The banquette is built-in under a bow window. *Photo courtesy of Lindquist & Co., Duluth, MN*

The banquette of cabinetry fills the corner. *Photo courtesy of Kitchen & Bath Design Consultants, LLC, West Hartford, CT*

135

This curved banquette is constructed from cabinetry. *Photo courtesy of Kitchens By Teipen, Greenwood, IN*

The banquette is built-in under the windows with materials that match the woodwork. *Photo courtesy of Northwoods Kitchens, Inc., Traverse City, MI*

Chapter 21

Pantries

Pantries provide extra storage for food items and for dishes and small appliances. They come in many sizes. The one shown with the heading for this chapter is even a separate room. Here are some other ideas for pantries.

Photo courtesy of Bella Domicile, Madison, WI and Brown House Design, Madison, WI

These pantries are only 12" deep. *Photo courtesy of The Kitchen Guide, Inc., Barrington, IL*

The kitchen has pantries both 24" deep and 12" deep for lots of extra storage. *Photo courtesy of Kichen Works, West Granby, CT*

The pantry cabinets provide additional storage. *Photo courtesy of Whole House Cabinetry, Inc., Glenmoore, PA*

The cabinets house a bar sink and extra storage. *Photo courtesy of DCI Home Resource, Charlotte, NC*

The open pantry shelves provide easy access to the items stored here. *Photo courtesy of Bella Domicile, Madison, WI*

The large walk-through pantry has a single sink, under counter refrigerator, microwave, and storage on both sides. *Photo courtesy of The Home Improvements Group, Woodland, CA*

The large pantry space has sink, microwave, dishwasher, under counter refrigerator, and lots of extra storage. *Photo courtesy of Jan Merrell Kitchens, Toledo, OH*

This pantry area has a sink and storage cabinets. *Photo courtesy of Bella Domicile, Madison, WI*

Chapter 22
Wine Storage

Wine storage ideas abound! There are many ways to keep a few wine bottles for immediate use that also add to the overall appearance of a kitchen. However, long-term wine storage is best done in a controlled temperature and humidity environment. The following are some examples of each type of wine storage.

Photo courtesy of Kitchen Places, Ventura, CA

Space is provided for a few bottles of wine in a row of cubbyholes under some of the wall cabinets. *Photo courtesy of DMR Remodeling, Inc., Park Hills, KY*

A vertical row of wine bottle cubbies are part of a wall cabinet. *Photo courtesy of Coastal Kitchen & Bath Designs, York, ME*

Double rows of wine cubbyholes in the cold center provides the storage.
Photo courtesy of Artisan Kitchen & Bath, San Jose, CA

Double columns of cubbyholes provide storage for a few bottles of wine.
Photo courtesy of Terra Nova Kitchen & Bath, Vienna, VA

A row of wine cubbyholes is provided as part of the island design. *Photo courtesy of Black Diamond Kitchens, Inc., Fraser, CO*

Two large "X" cubbyholes provide storage for multiple bottles of wine. *Photo courtesy of Northbay Kitchen, Petaluma, CA*

Storage is provided by two vertical columns of wine cubbyholes at the end of the island. *Photo courtesy of Roomscapes, Laguna Niguel, CA*

Diagonal cubbies are at the back of this island. *Photo courtesy of Carmike Kitchens, Mechanicsville, MD*

A base cabinet with round cubbies houses wine bottles. *Photo courtesy of Intercoastal Kitchen & Bath, Naples, FL*

A single column of wine cubbies is in addition to a wine refrigerator. *Photo courtesy of The Cabinet Works, Stratham, NH*

Wine bottle storage is provided by columns of cubbies in both wall and base cabinets. *Photo courtesy of Whole House Cabinetry, Glenmoore, PA*

Diagonal cubbies above the refrigerator provide storage for a few bottles of wine. *Photo courtesy of Whole House Cabinetry, Glenmoore, PA*

A wine refrigerator is at the end of an island. *Photo courtesy of Classic Kitchen & Bath, Roslyn, NY*

A wine refrigerator is in the upper part of the refrigerator behind the glass door. *Photo courtesy of Wellesley Kitchens, Inc., Wellesley, MA*

A full height wine refrigerator stores wine at controlled temperatures for long term storage. *Photo courtesy of Lang's Kitchen & Bath, Newtown, PA*

Full height vertical cubby holes provide storage for many bottles of wine. *Photo courtesy of Modern Millwork, Belleville, NJ*

Chapter 23

Accessory Cabinets

We end our journey into kitchen design by looking at some accessory cabinets. These are cabinets that match the kitchen cabinets, but are not part of the work centers. We include some well-designed hutches, bars, desk areas, etc.

Photo courtesy of Better Kitchens and Baths, Ventura, CA

A hutch provides space for the small TV. *Photo courtesy of Atwood: Fine Architectural Cabinetry, Birmingham, MI*

The hutch provides lots of display space as well as storage. *Photo courtesy of The Kitchen Guide, Inc., Barrington, IL*

The accessory cabinets provide desk space that can be hidden away behind retractable doors. *Photo courtesy of Blossom Brothers, Inc., Delray Beach, FL*

The cabinets frame the door in addition to providing dish storage. *Photo courtesy of Classic Kitchen & Bath, Roslyn, NY*

The cabinets provide display space and storage. *Photo courtesy of Mark Klevan Cabinetry, Stamford, CT*

The contemporary hutch contains some wine storage as well as display space and lots of closed storage.
Photo courtesy of Kuche + Cucina, Paramus, NJ

The accessory cabinets feature a wet bar and a small desk. *Photo courtesy of Kitchens By Teipen, Greenwood, IN*

A large desk area and display type hutch are adjacent to the main kitchen. *Photo courtesy of Bella Domicile, Madison, WI and Brown House Design, Madison, WI*

The cabinets house a wet bar with additional storage. *Photo courtesy of Southern Kitchens, Inc., Alexandria, VA*

The cabinets provide storage and display space. *Photo courtesy of The Cabinetworks, Stratham, NH*

Contributors List

A Kitchen & Bath Company
8442 Woodland Road
Millersville, MD 21108
410-544-5554
kathleen@akitchenandbathcompany.com
Sec. I, Ch.4, 8

All Trades Contracting, Inc.
P.O. Box 5411
Clinton, NJ 08809
908-713-1584
ray@alltradescontracting.com
Ch. 9

Apex Industries LLC
152 Darby Circle
St. Simons Island, GA 31522
912-222-6435

Appliance Associates of Buffalo
200 Amherst Street
Buffalo, NY 14207
716-873-4100
applianceassoc@aol.com
Ch. 9, 10, 14, 15

Architectural Kitchenworks
450 Schrewsbury Plaza #306
Schrewsbury, NJ 07702
732-915-7526
Ch. 7, 12

Artisan Kitchen & Bath
1456 Oak Canyon Court
San Jose, CA 95120
408-852-0050
tony.young@artisankitchenbath.com
Ch. 12, 22

Atlantic Coast Kitchen & Bath of Jacksonville
20 Blanding Road
Orange Park, FL 32073
904-272-2252
mark@ackb.com
Ch. 12, 16

Atwood: Fine Architectural Cabinetry
430 N. Old Woodward
Birmingham, MI 48009
248-203-2050
kris@atwoodcabinetry.com
Ch. 12, 13, 23

Bel Air Construction, Inc.
1655 Robin Circle
Forest Hill, MD 21050
410-557-9838
michael@belairconstruction.com
Ch. 3,6

Bella Domicile
P.O. Box 44189/6210 Nesbitt Road
Madison, WI 53744
608-271-8241
dluck@belladomicile.com
Ch. 1, 6, 8, Sec III, 13, 14, 15, 16, 18, 19, 21, 23

Bertch Manufacturing
4747 Crestwood Dr.
Waterloo, IA 50702
319-296-2987
Ch. 15

Better Kitchens & Baths
1884 Eastman Ave #106
Ventura, CA 93003
805-644-5844
mstanfordbkb@sbcglobal.net
Ch. 5, 12, 23

Black Diamond Kitchens, Inc.
P.O. Box 610
Fraser, CO 80442-0610
970-726-2888
jbarna@blackdiamondkitchens.com
Ch. 1, 9, 12, 16, 22

Blau Bath & Kitchen (C. B. Designs of NC)
604 Jimmies Creek Dr.
New Bern, NC 28562
252-636-3335
Ch. 5, 18

Blossom Brothers, Inc.
2706 North Federal Hwy.
Delray Beach, FL 33483
561-274-7020
info@blossombrothers.com
Ch. 6, 8, 23

Bourgeoisie, Inc.
601 South Cedar St. #205-D
Charlotte, NC 28202
704-372-9300

Brown House Designs
202 West Gorham St.
Madison, WI 53703
608-663-5100
Ch. 1, 21, 23

Builder Specialties
92 River St.
Montpelier, VT 05602
802-223-5583
matt@builderspecialties.com
Ch. 8, 9

Bytner Design Associates
20 W. Washington, Suite 6-A
Clarkston, MI 48346
248-922-0065
bytner@ameritech.net
Ch. 1, 2

Cabinet Tree, The
8602 Farmington Blvd, Suite 1
Germantown, TN 38017
901-854-7881
pntl@bellsouth.net
Ch. 12

Cabinet Source
2619 - A Executive Place
Biloxi, MS 39531
228-385-8880
appraiser300@belsouth.net
Ch. 14

Cabinetworks, The
118 Portsmouth Ave., Bldg. B-Suite 101A
Stratham, NH 03885
603-772-2128
thecabinetworks@ttlc.net
Ch. 4, 9, 11, 12, 15, 18, 22, 23

Callen Construction
S63 W 13131 Janesville Road
Muskego, WI 53150
414-529-5509
francis.jones@callenconstruction.com
Ch. 6, 10

Carmike Kitchens
41455 Queens Landing Road
Mechanicsville, MD 20659
301-475-9616
kinsey1@carmikekitchens.com
Ch. 14, 15, 22

Cassedy & Fahrbach
P.O. Box 788
Pittsboro, NC 27312
919-542-2578
pierce@cassedyandfahrbach.com
Ch. 12

Cederberg Kitchens & Additions
630 Weaver Dairy Road
Chapel Hill, NC 27514
919-967-1171
info@cederbergkitchens.com
Ch. 15, 16, 20

Charlestowne Kitchen & Bath
1519 Main St.
St. Charles, IL 60174
630-377-7878
bob@ctkb.com
Ch. 6, 10

City Kitchens
438 Massachusetts Ave.
Cambridge, MA 02139
617-864-3300
mike@city-kitchens.com
Ch. 6, 15

Classic Kitchen & Bath
1062 Northern Blvd.
Roslyn, NY 11576
516-621-7700
aboico@classick.com
Ch. 4, 5, 12, 13, 17, 18, 19, 22, 23

Coastal Kitchen & Bath Designs
316 US Rt. 1, Ste. B
York, ME 03909
207-351-1555
mark@coastalkbd.com
Ch. 6, 7, 8, 10, 16, 17, 22

Columbine Kitchen & Bath
309 Third Street
Castlerock, CO 80104
303-688-4199
richckb@qwest.net
Ch. 1

Country Cabinets, Etc.
Box 3240, 95 East Conway Rd.
North Conway, NH 03860
603-356-5766

ccetc@adelphia.net
Ch. 1, 2, 12, 16

Country Cupboards
36 Massa Drive
Kingston, NY 12401
845-382-2888
bill@country-cupboards.com
Ch. 11, 15, 17

Custom Crafters, Inc.
4000 Howard Ave.
Kensington, MD 20895
301-493-4000
cchwastyk@customcraftersinc.com
Ch. 7, 8, 17, 19

Custom Design
P.O. Box 1940
Oakhurst, CA 93644
559-683-2786
customdesign@sierratel.com
Ch. 14

DCI Home Resource
1300 South Blvd. Suite C
Charlotte, NC 28203
704-926-6000
carol.lindell@dcihomeresource.com
P. 4, Ch. 2, 6, 7, 8, 9, 10, 12, 21

Detailed Builders Inc.
417 N Quentin Rd.
Palatine, IL 60067
847-352-1800
rick@distinctivedesignbuild.com
Ch. 10, 19

DMR Remodeling, Inc.
1326 Amsterdam Road
Park Hills, KY 41011
859-261-9848
dmrremodel@juno.com
Ch. 9, 22

Expressions Kitchen & Bath Design Studio
615 Boston Post Rd. 2nd Floor
Sudbury, MA 01776
978-443-2546
altheaclark@verizon.net
Ch. 13

F&W Kitchens & Baths
42210 Cook Street, Suite J
Palm Desert, CA 92211
760-568-9673
jandrews@francisandwane.com
Ch. 4

Finial Properties
1007 Curtis St. Suite 1
Downers Grove, IL 60515
630-887-7964
dale@finialproperties.com
Ch. 18

Gilman Screens & Kitchens
228 Bayshore Blvd.
San Francisco, CA 94124
415-550-8848
larry@gilmanscreens-kitchens.com
Ch. 10, 13

Home Improvements Group, The
440 Main St.
Woodland, CA 95695
530-666-5061
kitrmdl@sbcglobal.net
Ch. 2, 5, 10, 12, 16, 17, 21

Homewood Kitchen & Bath, Inc.
18027 Dixie Hwy.
Homewood, IL 60430
708-799-0176
jackl8027@aol.com
Ch. 10, 11

Intercoastal Kitchen & Bath
4951 Tamiami Trail N #3
Naples, FL 34103
239-261-0346
johnmcmullin@softhome.net
Ch. 9, 22

Interstate Custom Kitchen & Bath, Inc.
558 Chicopee St.
Chicopee, MA 01013
413-532-2727
jim@interstatekitchens.com
Ch. 2, 5

J. B. Turner & Sons
3911 Piedmont Ave.
Oakland, CA 94611
510-658-3441
jb_turner@pacbell.net
Ch. 4, 17

Jan Merrell Kitchens
901 Jefferson Avenue
Toledo, OH 43624
419-246-0991
jan@janmerrellkitchens.com
Ch. 8, 19, 21

Kennedy Kitchen Distributors
2763 S. 6th St.
Springfield, IL 62703

217-522-2284
bathandbrass@spring1.com
Ch. 1

Kitchen & Bath Concepts of St. Simons, Inc.
3609 Frederica Rd.
St. Simons Island, GA 31522
912-634-0328
wbburgess@hotmail.com
P. 2

Kitchen & Bath Design Studio, Div. Wagner Fabrication
551 Brick Road
West Salem, WI 54669
608-786-3845
emailkbs@aol.com
Ch. 7, 11

Kitchen & Bath Galleries
8411-107 Glenwood Ave.
Raleigh, NC 27612
919-783-8848
postmaster@kandbgalleries.com
Ch. 19

Kitchen and Bath Design Consultants, LLC
1000 Farmington Ave.
West Hartford, CT 06107
860-232-2872
lorey@KBDConsultants.com
Ch. 19, 20

Kitchen Classics by Custom Crafters
6023 Wilson Blvd.
Arlington, VA 22205
703-532-7000
customcrafters@erols.com
P. 3, Ch. 7, 19

Kitchen Concepts of Durango
329 S. Camino Del Rio Ste. A
Durango, CO 81303
970-259-9533
kcd@animas.net
Ch. 8, 9

Kitchen Concepts, Inc.
10868 Kenwood Rd.
Cincinnati, OH 45242
513-531-3838
patryan@one.net
Ch. 7, 11, 12, 13

Kitchen Gallery
1034 Woodland Ave.
Knoxville, TN 37917
865-524-3457
terry@kitchengallery.com
Ch. 7, 16

Kitchen Gallery Of Spring Grove
2404 Spring Ridge Dr. Suite C
Spring Grove, IL 60081
815-675-6900
kitchengallery@rsg.org
Ch. 3, 5, 13, 15

Kitchen Guide, Inc., The
25834 North Knollwood Drive
Barrington, IL 60010
847-487-7075
lj@kitchenguideonline.com
Ch. 4, 7, 8, 10, 11, 12, 15, 17, 18, 21, 23

Kitchen Places
4125 Market Street #1
Ventura, CA 93003
805-658-0440
kitchenplaces@sbcglobal.net
Ch. 17, 22

Kitchen Works
282 Hartland Rd.
W. Granby, CT 06090
860-653-0827
susanmcquillan@hotmail.com
Ch. 2, 9, 10, 11, 21

Kitchens & Baths, Linda Burkhardt
P.O. Box 2224
Montauk, NY 11954
631-668-6806
info@lindaburkhardt.com
Ch. 4, 8, 17

Kitchens By Teipen
1035 North State Road 135
Greenwood, IN 46142
317-888-7345
michael@kitchensbyteipen.com
P. 1, Ch. 2, 3, 5, 7, 10, 12, 14, Sect. IV, 20, 23

Kitchens By Wieland
4210 Tilghman Street
Allentown, PA 18104
610-395-2074
wiel-kit-bath@fast.net
Ch. 8

Kitchens Etc.
221 Worcester Rd.
Framingham, MA 01701
508-879-3377
kitchensetc221@aol.com
Ch. 7, 19

Kitchens Unlimited
3550 Summer Ave.
Memphis, TN 38122

901-458-2638
susan@kitchensunlimited.net
Ch. 7, 8, 10

Kuche + Cucina
489 Route 17 South
Paramus, NJ 07652
201-261-5221
a@kuche-cucina.com
Ch. 16, 23

Kuntriset Kitchens
5127 State Highway 12
Norwich, NY 13815
607-336-4197
kunkit@frontiernet.net
Ch. 12, 15, 20

L & S Interiors
427 S. Black Oak Road
Anaheim, CA 92807
714-998-8477
strodriguez@sbcglobal.net
Ch. 1, 18, 19

Lang's Kitchen & Bath, Inc.
9 Summit Square Center, RT 413 & 332
Newtown, PA 19047
215-860-4143
langskb@comcast.net
Ch. 18, 20, 22

Lemont Kitchen & Bath
106 Stephen St. Suite 101
Lemont, IL 60439
630-257-8144
gary@lemontkitchenandbath.com
Sect. II, Ch. 18, 19

Lifestyle Kitchen & Bath Center
10530 S. Parker Rd., Unit A
Parker, CO 80134
303-841-8899
tim@lifestylekitchenandbath.com
Ch. 12

Lindquist and Co.
926 E. 4th St.
Duluth, MN 55805
218-728-5171
lindco@charterinternet.com
Ch. 7, 20

Living Spaces Cabinet Design Studio, W&J K&B
2312 Becketts Ridge Drive
Hillsborough, NC 27278
919-732-6969
robfoles@yahoo.com
Ch. 1, 3, 4

Living Spaces Custom Design
350 E. Main St.
Batavia, OH 45103
513-735-2393
livingspaces@fuse.net
Ch. 6, 11, 12, 20

Low Country Kitchen & Bath
P.O. Box 24174
Hilton Head, SC 29925
843-689-2124
brentlckb@aol.com
Ch. 10

Mark Klevan Cabinetry
101 Dunn Ave.
Stamford, CT 06905-1112
203-329-9251
Ch. 5, 8, 11, 18, 23

Mary Laborde Interiors
105 Worthing Rd.
St. Simons Island, GA 31522
912-634-2224
mlinteriordesign@hotmail.com
Ch. 3

Modern Kitchen & Bath
2701 John R
Troy, MI 48083
248-528-1598
info@modernkitchen-bath.com
Ch. 10

Modern Millwork
624 Washington Ave.
Belleville, NJ 07109
973-759-5943
andy@modernmillwork.net
Ch. 22

Nordic Kitchens & Baths
4437 Veterans Blvd.
Metaire, LA 70006
504-888-2300
rlshaw@nordickitchens.com
Ch. 1

Northbay Kitchen
822 Petaluma Blvd N
Petaluma, CA 94952
707-769-1646
drc80@aol.com
Ch. 3, 5, 7, 16, 22

Northwood Kitchens, Inc.
10240 E. Cherry Bend Rd.
Traverse City, MI 49684
231-941-1470

northwood@chartermi.net
Ch. 16, 19, 20

Prescott Stone Fabricators, Ltd.
607 Ellis Rd. Bldg. 49-A
Durham, NC 27703
919-598-7509
info@tandckitchens.com
Ch. 12

R & R Remodelers Inc.
423 Hazel St.
Clifton, NJ 07011
973-546-1372
rfzckd@hotmail.com
Ch. 5, 8, 10

Rehm-Brandt's Design
413 Main Street
Bennington, VT 05201
802-447-7907
kelly@rehmbrandts.com
Ch. 5

Roomscapes, Inc.
23811 Aliso Creek Road, Suite 139
Laguna Niguel, CA 92677
949-448-9627
rnassetta@roomscapes.net
Ch. 4, 8, 14, 17, 22

Shelly Design
709 Mt. Moriah #106
Cincinnati, OH 45245
513-752-1606
ellen@shellydesigninc.com
Ch. 8, 13, 15

Solara Designs
81 Hillside Avenue
Williston Park, NY 11596
516-248-0606
solaradesigns@aol.com
Ch. 6

Southern Kitchens, Inc
2350 Duke Street, #A
Alexandria, VA 22314
703-548-4459
bobr@southernkitchens.net
Ch. 9, 15, 18, 23

Spacial Design
524 San Anselmo Ave., Suite 146
San Anselmo, CA 94960
415-457-3195
susan@spacialdesigns.com
Ch. 1, 6, 15

Terra Nova Kitchen & Bath
8032 Leesburg Pike
Vienna, VA 22182
703-761-0604
terranova3@verizon.net
Ch. 10, 22

The Kitchen Source
77 Connecticut
San Francisco, CA 94107
415-552-5700
joni@bathandbeyond.com
Ch. 8, 15, 16

Thomas Lewis & Co.
P.O. Box 917
Lyons, CO 80540
303-823-9616
Ch. 8

Trubilt Home Products, Inc.
44 Ryle Ave.
Paterson, NJ 07522
973-942-4455
joebobe@optonline.net
Ch. 7, 9, 10, 12, 15

T-Squared Studios
2918 Shoshone Trail
Lafayette, CO 80026
720-308-9181
tamara@goodkitchens.com
Ch. 4, 5, 8, 13

Washtenaw Woodwrights, Inc.
702 South Main Street
Ann Arbor, MI 48104
734-994-8797
brucecurtis@woodwrights.com
Ch. 8, 18

Wellesley Kitchens, Inc.
398 Washington St.
Wellesley, MA 02181
781-237-5973
mpeckham@wellesleykitchens.com
Ch. 13, 15, 22

Whole House Cabinetry, Inc.
2948 Conestoga Rd.
Glenmoore, PA 19343
610-458-4428
wholecab@hotmail.com
Ch. 1, 4, 8, 12, 21, 22

Wood-Stock Kitchens
27 Park St.
Essex Jct., VT 05452
802-878-5333
wood-stock.kitchens@verizon.net
Ch. 2, 6, 13